BASICS OF MOTOR SKILLS

Developmental Activities for Kids

by Heather Greutman

Copyright © 2017, Heather Greutman - Growing Hands-On Kids, LLC

www.GrowingHandsOnKids.com

All rights reserved. This book or any portion thereof may not be reproduced or used in any manner whatsoever without the express written permission from the author except for the use of brief quotations in a book review.

Edited By: Shelley Brewer
Shiny WordWorks
https://www.ShinyWordWorks.com/

Design and Cover Art by: Cassondra Freeman
Beyond The Blogger
http://www.BeyondTheBlogger.com

Disclaimers

Heather Greutman is a Certified Occupational Therapy Assistant. This book is for educational use only. The advice and tips given are not a replacement for medical advice from a physician or pediatrician. Please consult their advice if you suspect any medical or developmental delay with your child. This book and tips do not replace the relationship between therapist and client in a one-on- one treatment session with an individualized treatment plan based on their professional evaluation. Please seek out your local Occupational Therapist for an evaluation if you suspect any delays in fine motor skills or other skills with your child.

All activities are designed to be completed with adult supervision. Please use your judgment when setting up these activities for your child and do not provide items that could pose a choking hazard for young children. Never leave a child unattended when completing any of these activities. Please also be aware of all age recommendations on the products you are using with your child. The author is not liable for any injury caused to your child while completing any of these activities.

What Other's Are Saying About This Book

"Watching your child struggle with any task can lead you to feel frustrated and helpless. As a parent, I know the feeling well. Thankfully, caring and knowledgeable therapists like Heather Greutman have provided amazing resources for us. It's important to understand why children struggle with daily living skills in order to provide the proper tools to help them. That's what I strive to do in my Pocket Occupational Therapist book series. Reading a book and gaining an immediate understanding of HOW to help your child leaves parents feeling empowered. Fine motor skills are critical to daily function and Heather gives readers a step-by-step map to ensure success for children. I highly recommend Basics of Fine Motor Skills to every parent and therapist."

- Cara Koscinski, MOT, OTR/L
The Pocket Occupational Therapist, www.PocketOT.com

"Basics of Fine Motor Skills" is an amazing resource for parents, therapists, and educators. I love the way Heather Greutman explains fine motor development in easy to understand terms, with simple explanations and descriptions. The activities are broken down by category as well as age, making it a go-to resource for any adult seeking to help the child in their life. I really appreciate the parent-friendly break down of developmental red flags, reflex integration, and fine motor friendly toys. This is definitely a resource that I'll be recommending to my readers. "Basics of Fine Motor Skills" is an incredible tool providing invaluable information for anyone seeking guidance to help their child. I will consider it a must-have in my OT resource library."

- Jaime Spencer, MS, OTR/L
Miss Jaime OT, www.MissJaimeOT.com

"Too many parents do not understand the importance of fine motor skill development in their Little Learners. They quickly dismiss "handwriting" as a lost and un-needed art. Heather's book shines a bright light on the fundamentally necessary motor skill development that is required for all children despite today's increasingly technological environment."

- April Whitlock, CEO
Fundanoodle

"This book is an amazing resource for parents, teachers, and therapists. Heather clearly explains everything you need to know about fine motor skills from babies up through young children. Her suggestions for activities and games in this book are so helpful and fun for children. This resource is jam-packed with valuable information and I highly recommend it!"

- Angela Thayer
Teaching Mama, www.TeachingMama.org

TABLE OF CONTENTS

7	Introduction
9	Importance of Fine Motor Skills
11	Early Skills Needed for Fine Motor Skills
12	- Importance of "Tummy Time"
13	- Involvement of Primitive Reflexes
16	- Importance of Crawling
18	Gross Motor Skills Involvement
19	- Crossing Midline
19	- Bilateral Coordination
20	- Motor Planning
21	- Muscle Tone
22	- Core Strength
23	Visual Motor Skills
24	- Visual-Perceptual Skills
24	- Eye-Hand Coordination
25	- Visual Motor Integration
27	Sensory Processing Skills
29	- The 8 Senses
30	- Senses that Affect Fine Motor Skills
33	Developmental Milestones
40	Fine Motor Development Red Flags
41	- Tests to Consider for Fine Motor Skills
42	- Common Diagnoses

47	Fine Motor Skills & Handwriting
51	Fine Motor Tools and Games
55	Activity Ideas by Skills
56	- Warm-up Activities
58	- Body Awareness Activities
59	- Bilateral Coordination Activities
60	- Crossing Midline Activities
61	- Shoulder and Postural Stability Activities
63	- Visual Motor Skill Activities
63	- Grip Strength
64	- Pinch Strength
64	- Finger Dexterity
65	- Pre-Writing Skills
67	Activity Ideas by Age
68	- Activity Ideas Ages 0-3
68	- "Tummy Time" Activities
69	- Fine Motor Activities for Ages 0-2
69	- Fine Motor Activities for Ages 2-3
71	- Activity Ideas for Ages 3-6
71	- "Tummy Time" Activities for Preschoolers
72	- Activities for Children who Skipped Crawling
73	- Fine Motor Activities for Ages 3-6
74	- Activity Ideas for Ages 6+
76	Final Thoughts
77	Glossary of Terms
82	Resources
86	Research Citations
88	About the Author

Introduction

Have you ever thought about how many times you use your hands during the day? Writing, typing, driving, dressing, feeding, even connecting with those around you use your hands. Imagine being unable to use your hands for one day. Even getting out of bed would be a challenge.

Often times we complete these daily tasks without even thinking about it because they become like second nature. Every single task you do takes fine motor skills and it is these all important skills that are the focus of this book.

Fine motor skills are extremely important for healthy childhood development. Not only does a child need to develop vital life skills such as bathing, dressing, eating and handwriting, these skills are part of their overall healthy development in other areas such as gross motor skills.

All these skills are connected, developing together and in partnership. Gross motor skill strengths and weaknesses impact growth in the fine motor areas. Core strength, bilateral coordination, crossing midline, and neck and shoulder strength are needed in order for fine motor skills to flourish.

Research even suggests that fine motor skills are so important that they are connected to how a child learns to read, complete math problems and other higher level cognitive thinking. (Clark, 2010). Isn't the brain an amazing thing?

In this book, we will take a look at all the skills needed to encourage good fine motor development in children between the ages of newborn to 6 years old. These ages are also when hands-on activities are most helpful. Children learn through movement, touching and feeling the world around them.

Whether you are a parent of a typically developing child or child with special needs, a teacher, or a therapist, this book will give you a good overview of what a child needs to develop strong fine motor skills.

Many of the activities in this book are multifaceted and designed to provide growth and benefits in a variety of growth areas, not just fine motor skills. It's important to keep these skills in the context of the big picture and the development of the whole child. We cannot focus on one set of skills at the exclusion of others. By bringing them all together, we can promote healthy development of the whole child. These activities are designed to engage children by being fun and encouraging the hands-on experiences that children this age crave.

My hope is that this book becomes your go-to resource for learning about fine motor skills and getting ideas for fun ways to incorporate them into your little learner's day.

PREFACE
Importance of Fine Motor Skills

In this age of technology, many Occupational Therapists in particular are noticing a lack of fine motor skills in young children. Referrals for children who lack the basic skills needed to use scissors or hold a pencil have seen a huge increase. When a child enters the Kindergarten environment, there are many basic fine motor skills they need in order to be successful. Unfortunately, many children are reaching Kindergarten lacking these basic areas.

Recent research even suggests that fine motor skills and executive function skills have an impact on future cognitive skills such a math, reading, and other learning skills. In a research article titled "Fine Motor Skills and Executive Function Both Contribute to Kindergarten Achievement." (Child Development, April 26, 2012) the researchers found the following:

> *"Notably, this study found that how well children could copy designs such as shapes was as important as their executive function for explaining their achievement in early literacy and comprehension.*
>
> *Overall, findings highlight fine motor competence as a unique skill associated with improved kindergarten entry performance and learning over the year in a variety of academic domains. Increasing children's opportunities for fine motor learning experiences with elements of copying designs may be one direction for curriculum supplements in early childhood."*

It has been suggested that there are many reasons for these lack of skills: decreased time outdoors, increased use of screen time and decreased tummy time. Children just aren't exposed to many of the activities they need in order to develop their core and hand strength like they were, even 20 years ago.

Fine motor skills involve developing and using the small muscles of the hands, forearm, arm, and shoulder in order to complete a variety of skills. You may not think that your baby picking up a toy and banging it is that important, but they are building the basis of their future success with fine motor skills.

CHAPTER 1

Early Skills Needed for Fine Motor Development

How can you, as a parent, or teacher, or therapist encourage these basic fine motor skills? Let's begin by taking a look at each building block needed for basic fine motor skill development. It all begins right after a baby is born.

Importance of Tummy Time

Allowing babies to have ample floor time and tummy time to explore the world around them is so important for their core, neck, and shoulder strengthening. Those early days have long ranging impacts with effects that are evident for years.

When a baby is young, there are specific motor and visual motor developmental milestones that are important to their overall development. Some of these milestones include the baby being able to lift and support its own head and neck against gravity, weight shifting up and over their body onto their hands and arms, and discriminating between things close and far away.

Once a child masters those areas, they start to build strong abdominal muscles that allow them sit up, stand, and eventually walk. From there they learn to weight shift on just their legs, and how to track objects with their eyes. Once they have developed these core muscles, all other positioning they need to sit for school activities comes easier and more natural.

Some basic skills that tummy time helps to develop are:

- Crawling and scooting which leads to walking.
- Balance and coordination (which helps them in play and exploring their environment).
- Eye-hand coordination (writing, visual/motor skills, scissor skills).
- Confidence and independence.

Once in school, a child who lacked sufficient tummy time as an infant may display the following struggles:

- Unable to concentrate (fidgeting, hyperactive).
- Poor eye tracking (teachers may complain that the child does not seem to listen when they are up front or walking around the room giving directions).
- Difficulty in gross motor tasks (clumsy or uncoordinated in gross motor play or poor desk posture such as resting their head on their arm or on the desk).
- Difficulty crossing the midline of the body. Using the right hand for objects on the right side of the body, left hand for the left side of the body.
- Difficulty with fine motor tasks, particularly with pre-writing lines and following lines, circle shapes, etc.
- For Therapists – STNR and ATNR reflexes still present in gross motor tasks (not integrated).

Involvement of Primitive Reflexes

In a baby's first few months of life, they have automatic, protective reflexes to sensory stimuli. Many of these reflexes also help babies to develop gross motor skills such as rolling or reaching for objects.

You may see these referred to as primitive reflexes. These reflexes are a critical part of a developmental sequence that is in place until mature postural reflexes to take over. Sometimes these primitive reflexes do not integrate (or disappear) which can lead to many developmental delays related to diagnoses like ADHD, sensory processing disorder, Autism and other learning disabilities.

If primitive reflexes are not integrated it affects a child's balance, sensory perceptions, fine motor skills, sleep, immunity, energy levels, impulse control, concentration, social, emotional and intellectual learning.

There can be many causes for retained primitive reflexes, some of these include a traumatic birth, birth by c-section, falls, trauma, lack of tummy time, delayed or skipped creeping and crawling, chronic ear infections (this affects balance in the inner ear), and head traumas.

Here is a basic overview of the reflexes that are related to future posture and fine motor skills.

The Rooting Reflex (also known as the sucking reflex) is when you touch a baby's cheek and they begin to suck. This allows the baby to breastfeed appropriately because it helps the baby to turn its head and suck at the breast. This reflex should disappear or integrate at around 4 months old. If this reflex does not integrate, you may notice difficulty with going to solids, poor articulation in speech, and thumb sucking.

The Startle Reflex is a primitive fight or flight response for a baby. It is noticeable when a baby thinks it is falling or feels a sudden lack of support. It involves three distinct movements which include the arms spreading out (abduction), bringing the arms back in (adduction) and crying. It typically integrates around 4 months old. If this reflex is retained, you may notice a child becoming over sensitive to incoming sensory input, sensory overload, poor impulse control, motion sickness, easily distracted, poor balance, poor coordination, unable to adapt to change and mood swings.

The Grasping Reflex (also known as the Palmer reflex) is when a baby's fingers automatically grasp an object (such as your finger). This reflex should integrate by 4 months, however if it does not you may notice difficulty with fine motor skills, sticking the tongue out while writing, or messy handwriting.

The Asymmetrical Tonic Neck Reflex (ATNR) is when a baby is lying on their back and as the head turns, the hand and leg on the side they are looking towards extends out, while the opposite side is pulled in. This reflex is the beginning of eye-hand coordination and should disappear by 6 months old. If this reflex does not integrate, the child may develop poor eye-hand coordination. Imagine trying to write and turning to look at something, but your hand pulls in while your other is reaching out. This affects posture during handwriting and other seated copying tasks in the classroom.

The Symmetrical Tonic Neck Reflex (STNR) or the crawling reflex, is a transitional reflex, which helps a baby to go from laying on the floor to creeping and crawling. You will notice this reflex briefly at birth, and then again before a child learns to crawl. It should disappear by 11 months old. It is one of the last reflexes to integrate, since all primitive reflexes should disappear by age 1. The STNR reflex divides the body in half at the midline. As the baby's head is brought to the chest, the arms and legs extend or push out. If this reflex is retained (or not integrated), you will notice slouched posture or the inability to sit still and concentrate. And now you get a small hint as to why crawling is such an important milestone.

So many reflexes play an important role in the healthy development of a baby. One of the most important is crawling, so let's talk about why it is such an important milestone now.

Importance of Crawling

Crawling is one of the most "essential developmental phases for optimal future learning." writes Sharon Promislow, an educational Kinesiologist and Educational Consultant. Not only does it strengthen the neck, arm, leg, and trunk muscles of a young child, but the mechanics of crawling actually stimulate different areas of the brain which influence the child's ability to learn.

In addition to promoting learning, it also encourages fine and gross motor skills by strengthening large and small muscle groups. This is especially important for shoulder stability and strength with fine motor skills and future handwriting.

Visual and tactile senses are stimulated and it helps with understanding language with both ears, instead of lying to one side with only one ear towards a noise. This helps to increase their visual and auditory learning skills.

Cross-lateral movement (using both sides of the body in coordinated movement) is improved and the ability to coordinate the arms, legs, hands, feet and eyes together. This enhances how children share and make sense of different sensory inputs from the body.

The most important reason is that the myelin, which is a substance that coats the nerves in the body, is produced the most when crawling. Myelin plays a critical role in the sending and receiving of the brains messages. More myelin means faster and clearer learning for your baby.

Most importantly, crawling is movement based learning, which is how all children are designed to learn. As a baby learns to crawl, it starts to use many transitional movements and positions. This helps a baby explore their world in ways they weren't able to previously. It also helps them perfect transitions between different movements and positions.

Crawling is the beginning stage of bilateral coordination, which is using both sides of the body together in coordinated movements. We'll be taking a closer look at bilateral coordination in the next chapter.

Gross Motor Skill Involvement

CHAPTER 2

Before fine motor skills can develop, a child needs strong core, neck, and shoulder muscles. When Occupational Therapists look at fine motor delays, they will look to see if the following gross motor skills are lacking.

Crossing Midline

Crossing midline is something that all of us do every day without even realizing it because it is an integrated movement from childhood. It is important for reading, writing, and many school activities.

What is midline? If you were to draw a line down the middle of your body, starting at the head, that is your midline. Every time you cross that line with either side of your body that is crossing midline. Crossing midline is a skill that children learn from infancy.

Crossing Midline Red Flags

Your child may actually "get stuck" in mid-reach. This may be evident in the need to switch hands to continue across the body, or they may compensate by moving their whole trunk to reach toward the opposite side. Poor mid-line crossing will affect how your child reads (tracking with the eye from left to right) and writes (using their dominate hand across starting at the left side of the paper and moving across the page).

Bilateral Coordination

Bilateral coordination is using both sides of the body together to perform different tasks. This includes things like using a rolling pin or alternating movements like climbing the stairs. You may also see the term bilateral integration to describe this skill. There are three ways that bilateral coordination skills are used in everyday activities.

First, symmetrical movements involve using each hand and each leg doing the same action at the same time such as rolling dough or clapping.

Reciprocal movements include actions where one hand or leg and then the other complete the same movement in a rhythmical way, such as peddling a bike.

Finally, lead hand and supporting hand movements include one hand completing most of the activity while the other supports. Both hands work together in a coordinated way. These skills include using scissors, threading beads, or lacing cards.

Bilateral Coordination Red Flags

Difficulties with bilateral coordination may result in a child having trouble tying their shoes, drawing, writing, crawling, walking, riding a bike, or they may just appear clumsy and uncoordinated. It also affects their visual motor skills, poor eye-hand coordination, fine motor skills, and issues with the vestibular system (or balance).

Motor Planning

Motor planning is an important skill to have when you come upon a new task that you have not completed before. Motor planning allows you to figure out how to complete this skill in the correct sequence from beginning to end. In order to do this, incoming sensory stimuli must be correctly read and organized, and the appropriate and coordinated motor responses used to complete the task.

Motor planning Red Flags

If a child is having difficulty with motor planning you will notice they get frustrated very easily when presented with a new task. They may say they "can't do it" or that it is "stuck", "broken", or "heavy". Of course, many children will say this as a behavioral reaction to just not wanting to do something. But in a child with poor motor planning, they really cannot figure it out and will be constantly frustrated with new tasks.

Muscle Tone

Muscle tone refers to the amount of tension you feel in your muscles when they are at rest. Muscle tone is working correctly when you are able to reach out to an object and efficiently bring to back to your body without any spills and with the proper amount of strength and grasp. You probably did it without even thinking about it, because you have normal muscle tone.

When a child has high or low muscle tone, this will greatly affect their movement and ability to use everyday objects in an efficient manner.

High tone means there is too much muscle tension at rest. The muscles are consistently tight and tense, even when a rest. You may notice this in a child who has contorted arms or legs due to cerebral palsy or other similar diagnoses. Often they need physical therapy to improve range of motion in the affected limbs.

Low tone means there is not enough muscle tension when the body as at rest. This child may appear to look "floppy" and they lack control when reaching for and grasping objects. They have difficulty grading their movements (or using the right amount of control) in order to perform that movement without spilling, knocking over, or breaking it.

Children with low tone will also have difficulties with posture, sitting upright, and lack of endurance. This has a direct impact on their ability to sit at a desk or table and complete fine motor activities.

Core Strength

Core strength involves the muscles of your abdomen, back, and pelvis. Core strength directly affects a child's ability to sit and move in and out of different positions in order to complete school work or other tasks.

In order for a child to have good core strength they need postural responses (moving the head and neck in order to change positions), balance responses (moving different areas of the body in order to maintain balance), and postural stabilization (maintaining an upright trunk position for extended periods of time).

Core Strength Red Flags

You may notice problems with a child core strength if the child has difficulty sitting upright for any period of time, difficulty with bilateral coordination activities, clumsy movement, difficulty with ball skills, running, jumping, and walking on rough ground or using stairs.

CHAPTER 3

Visual Motor Skills

Visual motor skills are when motor skills and vision (or eye-sight) work together to complete a task. It includes visual perceptual skills, functional visual skills, and eye-hand coordination in order to be efficient. Both systems, motor skills and vision, must be integrated for many fine motor and handwriting skills.

There are a few terms and skills that fall under visual motor skills, so let's take a look at those definitions.

Visual Discrimination

Visual discrimination is the ability to recognize visual images. It allows you to identify and recognize different shapes, forms, colors, objects, people, and printed materials.

Visual-perceptual Skills

Visual-perceptual skills are the ability organize and interpret visual information and give it meaning. This is needed for reading, spelling, math comprehension, and handwriting skills.

Functional Visual Skills

Functional visual skills are movements needed for a person to use their eyes. This includes eye movement, focusing, teaming (the ability of the eyes to work together) and alignment which affects depth perception or understanding where we are in relation to objects around us. All of these skills work together creating spatial awareness, or understanding where we are in space.

Eye-Hand Coordination

You may also see this referenced as hand-eye coordination. It involves coordinated control of eye movement with the hands in order to process visual input or information and to guide in reaching and grasping. Proprioception (one of the 8 senses we will talk about in the next chapter) is also needed in order for the hands to properly process information from the eyes.

Visual Motor Integration

Visual Motor Integration involves visual perceptual skills and ability to correctly perceive and replicate or copy shapes, lines, patterns, and pictures. In order for visual motor skills to integrate, a child needs a strong base of visual skills (visual perceptual, functional visual, and eye-hand coordination) and motor skills (shoulder stability, fine motor skills, and eye-hand coordination).

Visual Motor Skills Red Flags

Difficulty with the following skills may indicate a problem with visual motor skills.

- Tunnel vision (difficulty with peripheral awareness)
- Lazy eye
- Eyestrain
- Headaches
- Blurred or double vision
- Words running together when reading
- Difficulty with handwriting/spacing
- Covering or closing one eye
- Decreased reading comprehension
- Difficulty keeping attention on reading or writing activities
- Trouble copying from a board
- Avoidance of activities that are too close to the eyes
- Skipping over words/lines when reading
- Poor reading fluency

If you suspect any vision problems, it's important to have your child assessed by a developmental optometrist, or those that specialize in functional vision exams. Vision therapy programs can be extremely beneficial in getting the visual, sensory, and motor systems working together.

CHAPTER 4

Sensory Processing And Fine Motor Skills

I've mentioned a few of the sensory processing systems already in this book, but we need to take a closer look at them before we continue. Much of what we have learned goes back to incoming sensory input. If the sensory systems are not working together to read that sensory input correctly and respond appropriately, all the other skills we have talked about are affected.

The sensory system is basically comprised of the brain, spinal cord, and neurons. It is the neurological wiring by which we perceive and process sensory information coming from outside and even inside our bodies.

All the systems working together provide you with the "optimal level of arousal" which means you are able to perceive, process, and react to sensory stimuli and information in a timely manner.

When a person or child has sensory overload or low arousal, this is often referred to as sensory processing difficulties or sensory processing disorder. It basically means that their brains are "wired" differently and they have difficulty processing incoming sensory information.

You've probably heard of the typical 5 senses. But did you know there are really 8 sensory systems? Let's take a look at each one.

1. Touch/Tactile – This is often the most commonly recognized sensory system of the body and the one most people notice if they have an overactive or under-active tactile system. Anything you touch or feel is part of the tactile sensory system.

2. Hearing/Auditory – This includes hearing, listening, and being able to filter and selectively attend to auditory stimuli.

3. Sight/Visual – Using our eyes to see what is far or close to us. A typical person is able to use smooth and precise eye movements to scan and visually assess their environment.

4. Smell/Olfactory – When we eat we smell something first, if it smells good we are more likely to try it. If it smells bad that sends a warning that we may not like it OR that it is dangerous for us to eat. Smell travels directly to the emotional brain or the limbic system which is often why our emotions are tied to smells and foods.

5. Taste/Gustatory - The sense of taste involves the tongue and the ability to perceive taste and flavors. These flavors include salty, sweet, bitter, sour, and umami (or savory). The sense of taste is closely related to the sense of smell since we smell our food before we taste it.

6. Proprioception – This is one of the internal senses of the body that comes from the joints, muscles, ligaments, and other connective tissue. The proprioception system allows you to know where your body parts are in space and what they are doing without using your vision.

7. Vestibular Processing – The vestibular system is located in the inner ear and helps you to detect changes in regards to gravity. Are you sitting, standing, lying down, upside down, spinning, standing still etc? It is often referred to as the internal GPS system of your body.

It is the first system to develop in utero and the first sensory system to have a organized response to sensory input. It is located in the most protected area of the brain, and has a very close relationship to gravity, safety, survival, arousal, and attention. Vestibular processing is also closely linked to the proprioception, auditory, and visual senses of the body.

8. Interoception – This sense is all about the physiological condition of your body. Are you hungry, thirsty? Do you need to use the bathroom? Is your heart racing or at a normal pace? This sense is one that researchers are just finding out about, so much more research needs to be done to understand how it really works.

How Sensory Processing Affects Fine Motor Skills

Children who have sensory processing difficulties also often have decreased fine motor skills. Why is this and what is the correlation between the two?

Children with sensory processing difficulties and fine motor difficulties often lack the proper proprioceptive and vestibular input in order to function. They often appear to be uncoordinated, clumsy, or afraid of certain physical activities. As we saw in the chapter on gross motor involvement, these large muscle movements and skills are important for fine motor development. So if a child is struggling with sensory processing and not participating in the movement and gross motor activities they need to develop, fine motor skills can be lacking.

Sensory processing issues means that a child's brain has problems organizing all the information coming into the brain that it receives from the senses above. A child may not want to touch certain things or manipulate objects. Or certain sounds may hurt and they may avoid certain environments because of these sounds.

The two biggest senses that affect fine motor skills are proprioception and the vestibular system. As we saw above, proprioception is the sense of knowing where your arms and legs are in relation to your body and being able to move them appropriately without necessarily looking at them. Children with poor proprioception skills have to really think and concentrate on basic movement skills that you and I may not even think twice about.

The vestibular system affects their sense of balance and where they body is in space, eye movement, and spatial awareness. It really is the GPS of the body. If a child has difficulty with vestibular movements, they may feel off balance or out of control of their bodies.

Proprioception & Vestibular System Difficulties

A child with sensory processing problems with these two particular systems may seem awkward and clumsy. They may have difficulty walking up and down stairs because they don't know whether it's stable or not. They also tend to move slowly and avoid certain movement activities because they feel unfordable or scared.

They also may not know their own strength. This especially affects fine motor skills because they may not realize how much strength is needed to pick up an object like a pencil. This means they are putting too much pressure or too little pressure on objects and may either drop them or break items easily. They may rip a page or break a pencil.

They may try to avoid certain physical activities that would seem fun and most typical developing kids would enjoy. A swing may be a very scary activity for them because they are not processing the movement and feel off balance.

When a child has an under developed vestibular system, their brain is not getting the correct information from their eyes, ears, the sense of gravity or movement in their bodies. This is turn makes their brain and body feel unsafe. When they do not feel safe, their arousal level, attention, and survival mode responses kick in (fight or flight response).

They may also bump into things a lot or seem out of control of their bodies. This happens because they are not getting enough feedback from the sensory system and need to feel more movement to receive that input. They may knock into a wall or rub against the wall while walking down the hallway so they feel centered. They may also fidget with their legs while sitting in order to get that extra input their bodies are craving.

If you feel your child has sensory processing difficulties, it is best to talk to their doctor or school and ask for an Occupational Therapy evaluation. A therapist will be able to assess and find the appropriate activities or "sensory diet" that will help your child to process information throughout their day so they can function.

CHAPTER 5

Fine Motor Developmental Milestones for Ages

This list has been compiled from various sources and should not be used as a diagnostic tool. It is for educational and informational use only. If you do feel that your child has a delay in fine motor skills, please talk to your child's doctor and ask for a developmental evaluation or an evaluation by an Occupational Therapist.

The ages listed above each skill set is the average age range when these skills are mastered. All children develop at their own pace and may master these skills before or slightly after the age given.

The most important thing about this list is to understand what is age appropriate. You can use this as a guideline for knowing what types of skills to either encourage or challenge your child with at which age.

0-3 months old

- Hands are in a fisted position.
- Arm movements are random and not controlled.

- Will watch the movement of their hands and brings their hands to their mouth.
- Will swing at targets (toys, person) using their whole arm.
- Will follow a person's movements with their eyes (within a few inches from their face).
- Will begin to hold objects in their hands.

3-6 months old

- Reaches for toys using both arms.
- Begins to transfer objects from one hand to another.
- Holds hands together.
- Begins to notice objects a few feet away.

6-9 months old

- Begin to grasp and hold onto objects.
- Uses a raking grasp to move objects with fingers.
- Looking for one object while holding another.
- Pokes at objects using their index finger.
- Takes objects to their mouth.
- Explore textures and sensory input with the mouth.
- Begin to hold a bottle.
- Squeezes objects with their fist.
- Play with their own hands.

9-12 months old

- Begins to feed themselves finger foods.
- Will turn pages in a book a few pages at a time.
- Begins to put small objects in a cup or container.
- Pincer grasp develops (using index finger and thumb to grasp objects).
- Transfers objects between hands (beginning of crossing midline skills).

- Grabs crayons with a fisted grasp.
- Can hold two small objects in one hand.
- Begins to show a preference for one hand over the other (beginning development of right handed vs. left handed).

12 - 18 months old

- Can build a tower of 2 blocks high.
- Claps hands together (beginning of bilateral coordination).
- Waves goodbye.
- Can scoop objects with a spoon or small shovel.
- Bangs objects together using both hands (beginning of bilateral coordination).
- Puts small objects into a container.
- Scribbles with crayons on paper.

18 months - 2 years old

- Putting rings on pegs.
- Begins holding a crayon with finger tips and thumb.
- Can remove pegs from a pegboard.
- Marks or scribbles with a crayon or pencil.
- Can build a tower 3 to 4 blocks high.
- Can open loosely wrapped packages or containers.
- Begins to start cutting paper with scissors (closer to 2 years old).
- Can turn pages in a book one page at a time.

2 years old

- Manipulates clay or play dough.
- Can stack a block tower 9 blocks high.
- Can turn doorknobs.
- Can pick up small objects with pincer grasp (index finger and thumb).
- Can complete 3 piece puzzles.

- Makes scribbles on paper.
- Make snips on paper with scissors.
- Washes hands independently.
- Can screw lids on containers on and off.
- Can string large beads.
- Zips and unzips large zippers.
- Can use a spoon correctly.

3 years old

- Can draw a circle after being shown model.
- Cuts a piece of paper in half.
- Copies prewriting lines of vertical, horizontal, and circle shapes.
- Laces a card.
- Can unbutton large buttons.
- Can cut a long a wide line with 1/2" accuracy.
- Will string 1/2 inch beads.
- Sorts objects.

4 years old

- Can copy cross shapes, right and left oblique lines "/" "\", square and X shapes.
- Can touch the tip of each finger to their thumb.
- Can color within a picture with no more than 1/4" deviations from the coloring lines.
- Can cut big circles with scissors.
- Can move the paper while cutting along a line.
- Completes puzzles of 4-5 pieces.
- Can use a fork correctly.
- Can get dressed and undressed without help.
- Uses dominate hand.
- Cuts along a line with no more than 1/8-1/4 inch deviation from the line.
- Will fasten and unfasten large buttons.

5 years old

- Grasps a pencil correctly.
- Begins to print their name.
- Copies a triangle shape.
- Cuts out a circle.
- Opens a lock with a key.
- Draw a diamond shape when given a model.
- Draws a person with at least 6 different body parts.
- Can tie their shoes.

6 years old

- Can copy first name.
- Builds a small structure with blocks.
- Can put a 16-20 piece puzzle together.
- Uses a knife to cut food.
- Cuts well with scissors, no deviations from the cutting line.
- Prints 3 or more simple words.
- Can print all numbers 0-9.
- Can print all letters of the alphabet, upper case and lower case.

Ages 6+

- Fully developed eye-hand coordination.
- Use all eating utensils appropriately.
- Help with household chores (sweeping, moping, dusting etc).
- Able to take care of pets (feeding, grooming, walking etc).
- Draw detailed and complex shapes or pictures.
- Begin to develop writing and handwriting habits and skills.
- Can compete in sports activities appropriately.
- Have hobbies they enjoy and complete independently.
- Learn a musical instrument.

- Begin computer skills and use video games.
- Are able to draw with greater control and precision.
- Ride a two-wheeled bike.
- Learning swimming skills.
- Move in time to the beat or rhythm of music.
- Able to twist and spin in one place.
- Are able to combine motor skills such as running and kicking or moves to music.

CHAPTER 6

Fine Motor Development Red Flags

One question many parents or teachers have in regards to fine motor skills is when to be concerned about delays. It is important to remember that the typical fine motor developmental can happen at a range of ages and all children develop at different paces.

However, there are some things that can be red flags in regards to fine motor skill development:

- Showing no interest is grasping objects
- Poor eye-hand coordination and seem excessively clumsy
- For school age children, they tend to avoid quiet, sit down activities such as drawing or writing
- Difficulty using utensils for eating
- Difficulty using their hands for basic activities such as building blocks or scribbling on paper
- Difficulty riding a bike or throwing a ball
- Difficulty with handwriting or writing skills (like holding a pencil)
- Sequencing the appropriate muscle movements for an activity (ex. opening a door, taking out a coat, putting the coat on)
- Tests to Consider for Fine Motor Skills

Most of these standardized assessments need to be administered by a licensed professional or therapist, they are not for parent or teacher use. However, it is important to be informed about the testing procedures and outcomes so you can successfully advocate for your child.

Note, there may be other informal tests a therapist may choose to use, but these are the formal assessments used by most.

The Beery-Buktenica Test (also known at the VMI or Developmental Test of Visual-Motor Integration) is for people ages 2 through adulthood. It helps to identify problems with visual perception, fine motor skills (especially hand control) and eye-hand coordination. The short form test (for ages 3-8 years old) contains 15 figures that the person needs to copy without erasing and without turning the booklet.

The long form test (ages 8 and above) contains 24 figures or shapes that need to be copied.

The Lincoln-Oseretsky Motor Development Scale looks at the development of motor skills in children ages 6-14 years old. It specifically looks at fine and gross motor skills, finger dexterity and speed, and eye-hand coordination. The test includes 36 tasks that progress in complexity. These tasks include walking backwards, standing on one foot, touching your nose, jumping over a rope, throwing and catching a ball, jumping and clapping, putting coins in a box and balancing on tiptoe while opening and closing your hands.

Peabody Developmental Motor Scale (PDMS-2) is designed for toddlers and preschool age children (ages 5 and under) to assess motor skill development. It looks at gross motor skills such as bending, balancing, crawling, walking, reflexes and jumping, and fine motor skills such as object manipulation, grasping, and visual-motor integration.

Brunininks-Oseretsky Test of Motor Proficiency (BOT-2) is a comprehensive test of gross motor and fine motor skills for children ages 4-21 years old. The short form test can be administered in 15-20 minutes, while the long form test takes 45-60 minutes. Some of the activities a child will perform include using manipulatives, balancing, running, push-ups, cutting paper, connecting dots, copying images, transferring pennies, sorting cards, stringing blocks, foot tapping, jumping jacks, single-legged hop, ball tossing, ball catching, and sit-ups.

Common Diagnoses with Fine Motor Skill Difficulties

There are some common diagnoses that often present with fine motor skill difficulties. It is important to know what they are, but you do need to have your child receive further testing to rule out or confirm these diagnoses.

Cerebral Palsy (CP) is a neurological disorder caused by non-progressive brain injury or malformation that occurs while the child's brain is under development (before birth, during birth, or right after birth). It primarily affects body movement and muscle coordination. This includes muscle control, muscle tone, reflexes, posture and balance, fine motor skills, and oral-motor functioning. It can also have other complications including intellectual impairment, seizures, and vision or hearing impairment.

Developmental Coordination Disorder (DCD - also known as Motor Skills Disorder or Motor Coordination Disorder) is when a otherwise healthy child can appear to be "clumsy" or forgetful. It may occur alone or with another diagnosis such as ADD/ADHD. Children have difficulty with sitting and walking and may find it hard to do simple motor tasks such as tying their shoes. Physical Therapy and Occupational Therapy are beneficial to help improve coordination.

Dyspraxia is a form of Developmental Coordination Disorder (DCD) that affects fine and/or gross motor coordination in children and adults. It can also affect speech. The cause of dyspraxia is unknown, however it is thought to be caused by a disruption in the way the brain sends messages to the rest of the body. This affects the child's ability to perform movements in a smooth and coordinated way. Dyspraxia refers to people who have difficulty with planning, organizing, and carrying out movements in the right order for everyday situations.

Dysgraphia is considered a learning disability and affects a child's handwriting and fine motor skills. They may have problems with illegible handwriting (print and cursive), inconsistent spacing, show inconsistencies such as a mixture of print and cursive letters, or upper and lower case lettering, strange wrist, body or paper orientation, poor spatial planning on paper, poor spelling, and difficulty with composing writing as well as writing and thinking at the same time. They may complain of a sore hand when writing or use an unusual grip.

Developmental Delays are when a child's development has any significant lag in their physical, cognitive, behavioral, emotional, or social development compared to normal developmental milestones. This term is only used for children from birth to age 3. After age 3, other age appropriate diagnoses may be given based on the child's specific delays.

Traumatic Brain Injury (TBI) is when an external physical force causes total or partial functional disability or psychosocial impairment that affect the child's educational performance. It can affect areas such as cognition, language, memory, attention, reasoning, abstract thinking, judgement, problem solving, sensory, perceptual and motor abilities.

Attention Deficit/Hyperactivity Disorder (ADD/ADHD) affects a child's ability to focus and sustain attention. They also show hyperactivity and impulsive behavior. They can also struggle with low self-esteem and often struggle in school with poor performance. There are three types of ADD/ADHD:

Inattentive - This is usually referred to as ADD, when a person is easily distracted and inattentive but not hyper or impulsive. They can be forgetful, fail to give close attention to school work, details, or make careless errors, have trouble keeping attention on task, ignores the speaker (even when spoken to) may not follow instructions and fails to finish school work or chores in a timely manner, and often loses focus or is easily sidetracked. Children also struggle with organization, dislike tasks that require them to put forth extended mental effort, such as homework. They can also lose important items such as their phone, wallet, books, or keys.

Hyperactive/Impulsive - A child will show signs of hyperactivity and impulsiveness but not inattention. They may appear to always be "on the go", talk excessively, severe difficulty waiting for their turn, squirm and fidget in their seats, tap their hands or feet, get up from their seat frequently, unable to quietly play or take part in a leisure or hobby, blurt out an answer before the question has been given, or intrude and interrupt others constantly.

Combined - This is a combination of the two above where a child shows signs of inattention, hyperactivity, and impulsiveness.

In order for this diagnosis to be made, a child must meet several symptoms above before the age of 12 years old and the symptoms are noticeable in different environments (such as at home, school, with friends, etc). Plus it needs to be shown that the symptoms clearly interfere with their functioning within those settings and they are not able to be explained by other conditions such as mood or anxiety disorders.

Autism Spectrum Disorder (ASD) presents with social, communication, and behavioral challenges. These can show as mild, moderate, or severe and include Autistic Disorders, Asperger's Syndrome, and Pervasive Developmental Disorder. Signs of ASD include:

- Not pointing at objects to show interest.
- Not looking at objects when another person points at them.
- Having trouble relating to others or do not have an interest in other people at all.
- Avoiding eye contact and wanting to be alone.
- Having trouble understanding other people's feelings or talking about their own feelings.
- Prefer not to be held or cuddled, or might cuddle only when they want to.
- Can appear to be unaware when people talk to them, but respond to other sounds.
- May be very interested in people, but not know how to talk, play, or relate to them.

- Repeating or echoing words or phrases said to them, or repeating words or phrases in place of normal language.
- Having trouble expressing their needs using typical words or motions.
- Not interested in playing "pretend" games (for example, feeding a doll or playing house).
- Repeating actions over and over again.
- Having trouble adapting when a routine changes.
- Having unusual reactions to the way things smell, taste, look, feel, or sound.
- They may lose skills they once had (for example, stop saying words they were using).

Most children are not diagnosed with Autism until age 2 or older, with severe cases being diagnosed much earlier (18 months old or younger).

If you do suspect your child has Autism, it is important to seek early intervention as soon as you can. Even if you do not have an official diagnosis, they may still qualify for services, which can help promote development and learning new skills. Early intervention is considered ages 0-3 years old. When a child turns age 3, they transition to school based services through a local district or preschool. If you have any questions about these services, talk to your child's pediatrician or contact your local early intervention center.

CHAPTER 7

Fine Motor Skills & Handwriting

I noticed some confusion on the difference between fine motor and handwriting skills when I was doing some research for this book. I decided to address this in a way that I hope makes sense and educates on which fine motor skills are needed to be successful in handwriting.

You have probably seen many news stories about how many children are now entering Kindergarten lacking in fine motor skills which significantly affects how they are able to participate in the classroom. Referrals to Occupational Therapy are up and many in the school system are noticing this overall lack of fine motor skills. It's important to remember that fine motor skills not only affect handwriting, but all classroom activities and skills. While handwriting tends to be where many notice a concern with fine motor skills, it is not the only red flag.

Handwriting is a complex language expression skill and involves the following areas:

- Knowing letters of the alphabet
- Visual perceptual skills
- Following a sequence
- Controlling the paper to stay within the lines
- Letter formation
- Understanding left to right progression
- Understanding top to bottom progression
- Tracking the movement of the hand, pencil and paper
- Crossing midline skills
- Bilateral coordination skills

In order to achieve mastery in handwriting gross motor skills, fine motor skills and visual motor skills need to be integrated.

Handwriting is such an important skill to have for future reading, communication and written expression. This is why it is important to make sure the building blocks for handwriting are solid.

While you do need a solid base of fine motor skills in order to complete handwriting tasks, they are not one in the same. Handwriting difficulties often stem from poor fine motor skills, there are also many other areas that therapists or teachers need to consider when addressing handwriting difficulties.

A very common issue with handwriting is an incorrect pencil grasp. It has been commonly believed that a poor pencil grasp leads to poor legibility in handwriting, however, some research suggests that there may not be a significant effect.

The most significant fine motor skill that can be connected directly to poor handwriting skills is in-hand manipulation. This refers to the skill of picking up an item and being able to move it around in your hand or manipulate it. In some studies, it appeared that in-hand manipulation skills had a significant effect on letter formation, which in turn had an effect on writing tests. The children with fine motor delays ended up needing more time and dropped items more frequently or required external help for stability in order to complete their writing tasks.

While strong fine motor skills are needed for a good pencil grasp, there could also be sensory concerns or visual motor concerns.

Proprioception is the sense of knowing where your body is in space and has a direct impact on the ability to know how much pressure to place on an item. This affects pencil grasp since a child that needs a higher amount of proprioceptive input, may not recognize how much pressure they are placing on a writing utensil.

Visual motor concerns with handwriting could include not knowing that all writing and reading starts from left to right and top to bottom. It is important to address these areas along with all fine motor activities.

It is also important to remember that children are still figuring out which hand is dominate between the ages of 2 and 4 and may not fully develop until age 6. Many are also not ready for handwriting until age 6 or 7. This will have an effect on how they hold the pencil, as the dynamic tripod grasp is not developmentally appropriate until age 4-6.

It is important to rule out all of these concerns when addressing fine motor skills, which is why it is important to have your child assessed by a professional, like an Occupational Therapist, so they can address all of these areas and find out what exactly could be causing your child's handwriting difficulties.

I am not going to be addressing handwriting skills directly, but many of the ideas and skills I talk about are important building blocks for future handwriting. Pre-writing skills are especially important at this age.

Handwriting is such a complex skill that it really takes a whole other book to address it. At the end of this book I provide a list of further reading on handwriting skills.

CHAPTER 8

Fine Motor Tools & Games

Before we move on to the different activity ideas and suggestions, I wanted to give you an idea of things to have on hand in your home in order to practice fine motor skills. Many of these items you may already have. I've also included some good games to look into that focus on the skills needed for fine motor development.

Fine Motor Tools

- Handy scoopers
- Gator grabber tweezers (or bubble tongs)
- Twisty droppers
- Squeeze tweezers
- Various wooden spoons
- Scooping bowls
- Fine motor tongs
- Hole punch
- Play dough (homemade or store bought)
- Nuts and bolts
- Clothes pins
- Squeeze bottles (such as old Ketchup or mustard bottles)
- Stickers
- Wikki Stix
- Squeeze ball
- Peg board and pegs
- Pom-poms
- Cotton balls
- Water dropper and/or turkey baster
- Glue sticks
- Glitter glue bottle
- Colored craft stick
- Velcro dots
- Glue dots
- Kwik Stix paint
- Beads and string for threading beads
- Kinetic sand

- Cookie cutters
- Wooden blocks to make designs
- Craft pipe cleaners
- Colander
- Child size cooking utensils
- Magnets
- Beads
- Buttons (various sizes)
- Toothpicks
- Circle cereal
- String for lacing or stringing activities
- Puzzles
- TheraPutty

Game Ideas

- Hand clapping games
- The Sneaky Snacky Squirrel Game

- Go Fish (or other card games)
- Jenga
- Peg Board Game - Fun Express
- Froggy Feeding Fun - Learning Resources
- Super Sorting Pie - Learning Resources
- Ring Toss Game
- Wooden Fishing Game - Melissa And Doug
- Hungry Dog Motor Skills Game - Lakeshore Learning Materials
- Fine Motor Fruit Sorting - Adapt Ease (Amazon)
- Hungry Monkey Motor Skills Game - Lakeshore Learning Materials
- Tangram Puzzles
- Pounding Bench with Wooden Toy Mallet - Melissa And Doug
- Thumbs Up! Dexterity Game

CHAPTER 9

Activity Ideas by Skills

This section is packed full of activity ideas to work on a certain aspects of fine motor skills. Remember all of these activities should be done with adult supervision and some items may be too small for children under 3 years old. Use your own discretion when doing these activities with younger children.

Warm-Up Activities

The following exercises will prepare a child for fine motor activities and handwriting. They are most effective when completed prior to any fine motor activity.

Shoulder Warm-Ups

Shoulder Shrugs

Shrug the shoulders forward, then backward.

Crocodile Snaps

Start with one arm straight above the head and the other extended down one side of the body. Then snap the hands together meeting above the head, like a crocodile snapping its jaws. Repeat reversing the arm positions.

Air-traffic Controller

Start with the elbows bent and the hands in a fist in front of each shoulder. Straighten the elbows moving one arm out to the front of the body and the other arm to the side of the body. Alternate movements.

Butterflies

Begin with the arms extended straight in front of the body. Link the thumbs to make an "x" and turn the palms to face out. Using the shoulder only, make small circles with the hands, moving the hands to the left and right in unison (the fingers should lie side by side and are not moving - the movement is coming from the shoulders).

Chair push-ups

Begin by sitting up straight in the chair with hands gripping the sides of the chair, thumbs facing forwards and the fingers pressing against the underside of the chair. Using the strength in the arms, push the bottom up from the chair. The feet should also come up off of the floor.

Desk push-ups

Start with the hands flat on the desk. Place the tips of the thumbs and index fingers facing each other to create a triangle. Bend the elbows to bring the nose towards the triangle and then push with the arms to straighten the elbows again.

Finger Warm-Ups

Put on imaginary writing gloves

Pretend to pull on gloves or mittens, applying firm pressure to the fingers and back of the palm of each hand. This exercise provides proprioceptive feedback and prepares the muscles for movement.

Spider Push-Ups

Place the finger tips together and bend and straighten the fingers while pushing the finger tips against each other.

Pencil Olympics

Twirl the pencil like a baton, spinning it both horizontally and vertically.

Inchworm

Using a tripod grip, move the fingers along the pencil from one end to the other. Do not use the other hand to help support the pencil.

Piano Fingers

Drum the fingers on a desk as if playing a piano. Make sure each fingertip touches the desk.

Body Awareness Activities

- Play with a large ball, encourage the child to kick the ball using one foot and then the other. Practice throwing and catching the ball.
- Encourage the child to ride a bike, push the bike or pedal the bike with or without side-wheels according to the child's ability.
- Play "Simon Says". Say those words and then do an action that the child must copy.
- To teach a child spatial relations, ask them to stand in front of a

chair, behind a chair, next to the chair, on top of the chair or crouch under the chair.
- Have the child be your shadow and mimic all your actions as you walk and perform simple actions (i.e. marching in place, cross crawls, bringing elbows to the knee, raising arms above the head etc).
- Learn action songs and perform the actions as you sing them.
- Ask the child to imitate the movement of different animals: slither like a snake, waddle like a duck, hop like a rabbit etc.
- Encourage them to balance on one leg, and then the other for as long as possible. Time them to see if they can beat their own best record!

Bilateral Coordination Activities

- Stencils - make sure they hold the stencil with one hand while tracing with the other hand.
- Hand clapping activities.
- Lacing activities - lacing cards or lace up stockings (two pieces of construction paper with holes punched around the edges).
- Liter tube - cut off the bottom of 2, two liter bottles. Stuff the bottles with crumpled colored paper. Use clear packing tape to connect wide ends of the bottle together. Have the child hold the "handles" with both hands. Toss crumpled paper or a soft ball for the child to hit with the liter tube.
- Games like Bop It, Mr. Potato Head (make sure the child stabilizes the head with one hand while placing body parts with the other hand), Rubik's cube, Etch-A-Sketch, rhythm sticks, and Legos° are all fantastic for practicing bilateral skills.
- Play Four Square - make sure the child uses both hands to bounce the ball.
- Ball and balloon games - have the child use both hands to pass the ball or balloon overhead, between legs, roll at a target etc.
- Scissor activities. Use one hand to hold and turn the paper, the other to cut.

- Pounding or hammer activities. Use one hand to stabilize, the other to pound. Encourage use of the dominate hand/arm for pounding.
- Roll dough with a rolling pin.
- Squeeze objects (i.e. glue bottles) with both hands.
- Use both arms to twirl streamers or scarves.
- Build with building blocks.
- Trace patterns on paper.
- Spread icing on cookies, cakes etc.
- Tear lettuce for a salad, tissue paper for crafts etc.

Crossing Midline Activities

- Play with rhythm scarves.
- Play with blocks (stacking).
- Dance to music.
- Use a washcloth to bathe.
- Dusting or sweeping the house.
- Playing patty-cake.
- Play with cars on a large path.
- Play flashlight tag.
- Wash the car.
- Paint with a large paint roll.
- Cross crawls (touching right hand to the left foot or knee and left hand to the right foot or knee).
- Wipe off the table with a towel or washcloth using one hand.
- Stepping with out to throw a water balloon
- Draw a large, horizontal figure 8 on a chalk board or sidewalk.
- Squirt/water gun target practice.
- Water flowers with a garden hose using both hands.
- Ball pass relay races.
- Bean bag toss while sitting crisscross applesauce.
- Play tennis.
- Play a game of "Simon says".

Shoulder and Postural Stability Activities

Often problems with handwriting are thought to be due to fine motor deficits. However, issues can stem from a variety of problems. This is why it is important to build strength and address deficits in gross motor skills, especially posture and shoulder stability. Once these are addressed, fine motor skills will be easier to improve.

- Activities that promote weight bearing through the arms and shoulders.
- Weight bearing through the arms and shoulders.
- Swinging between monkey bars or trapezes.
- Wheelbarrow walking.
- Crab-walking.
- Bear walking.
- Doing the inchworm (walk hands forward, then the hands stay still and the feet walk up to the hands and repeat).
- Push-ups.
- Shooting baskets with a basketball.
- Jumping rope.
- Egg relay races.
- Playing with a yo-yo.
- Making large circles or figure 8 shapes on a blackboard or white board.
- Any activities on a vertical surface.
- Donkey kicks - in the push-up position, keep both ankles together while jumping feet from right to left and back again.
- Pouring activities with water or a watering can.
- Push or pull a wagon.
- Make wood projects requiring sanding and hammering.

Complete Fine Motor Activities in a variety of positions:

- Standing at a chalkboard.
- Lying on their stomach on the floor.

- Kneeling at a work surface.
- Side-sitting on the floor.

Core Strengthening Exercises

- Sit-ups.
- Crunches.
- Leg lifts.
- Oblique or twist sit-ups.

Back exercises

- Scooter boards.
- Swings.
- Therapy ball activities.
- "Tummy time".

Hand and Finger Strength Activities

There are 25 muscles in the human hand. That's a lot of muscles that need to work together as a team to promote effective and efficient fine motor skills. Any weakness in these muscles and lead to problems.

- Use tweezers or chopsticks for picking up small objects.
- Pick up pom-poms with clothespins and transferring to a container.
- Use squirt bottles for a rubber duck race.
- Use a turkey baster to transfer water.
- Use a hand held hole punch for arts and crafts.
- Create with modeling clay or playdough.
- Tear paper while keeping the ring and pinky finger tucked into the palms.
- Stringing beads.
- Roll tissue paper into balls and use for collages or crafts.
- Roll a dice for a game.

- Shuffling cards.
- Using scissors.
- Lacing or threading activities - macaroni, straws, blocks, beads.
- Complete mazes.
- Dot-to-dots tracing over straight and curvy lines.
- Writing letters or numbers in shaving cream, finger paint, pudding, or sand.

Visual Motor Skill Activities

- Copy patterns or pictures using shapes, pegs or crayons.
- Put together models.
- Dot-to-dot pages.
- Complete mazes.
- Hidden picture search and find pages.
- Word searches.
- Put together puzzles.
- Lacing activities.
- Ring toss games.
- Practice cutting with scissors.
- Transfer objects with bubble tongs.
- Cut straws into small pieces and string to make a necklace.
- Cut playdough or putty.
- Cut out foam shapes.
- Cut pictures out of cereal boxes.

Grip Strength

- Squeeze putty, a flour sifter, or plastic squeeze bottles.
- Squeeze a turkey baster for activities with water or other liquids.
- Squeeze juice from lemons, limes, or oranges.
- Squeeze a spray bottle (to water plants, clean windows, spray designs in the snow).
- Stir batter in a bowl.
- Staple papers together with a small stapler.

- Use a hole punch to make dots or creative shapes.

Pinch Strength

- Peel stickers off of surfaces.
- Peel fruit (i.e. lemons, oranges etc.).
- Lock and unlock a keyed lock.
- Deal cards for a card game.
- Use tongs to pick up small objects (cotton balls, smaller erasers, pom-poms etc.).
- Spin tops.
- Play with wind-up toys.
- Tear paper (construction paper or tissue paper) for art projects.
- Build with small blocks.
- Roll small amounts of putty or playdough into balls between the fingers.
- Lace cards.
- Pick up small objects (i.e. beans, rice, cereal, corn kernels) with fingers and place in containers.
- Place coins into a bank with a small slit.
- Pop bubbles on bubble wrap.
- Use small rubber stamps to create a picture.
- String beads to make a necklace.
- Pinch clothespins (for laundry or games).

Finger Dexterity

- Press cookie cutters into dough or putty.
- Play with finger puppets.
- Screw and unscrew small lids or nuts and bolts.
- Fold paper (i.e. origami, airplanes etc.).
- Hold a handful of marbles, transferring one at a time into a container.
- Draw shapes and write words in a variety of mediums (i.e. shaving cream, sand, finger paint, hair gel in a baggie, etc.).

- Draw designs on an Etch-a-Sketch board.
- Play board games with small pieces to manipulate (i.e. Connect 4, Trouble, Chinese Checkers, Chess etc.).
- Use fingers to sprinkle toppings on food (i.e. sprinkles, shredded cheese etc.).

Pre-Writing Activities

This includes any activity that focuses on the pre-writing lines needed for future letter formation and handwriting skills.

Age appropriate pre-writing skills are:

- Vertical Line – (Age 2 imitates, age 3 copies/masters)
- Horizontal Line – (Age 2 1/2 imitates, age 3 copies/masters)
- Circle Shape – (Age 2 1/2 imitates, 3 copies/masters)
- Cross Shape (+) – (Age 3 1/2 imitates, age 4 copies)
- Square Shape – (Age 4)
- Right/Left Diagonal Line – (Age 4 1/2)
- X Shape – (Age 5)
- Triangle - (Age 5)

Activity Ideas:

- Use a paintbrush in sand
- Use a finger in shaving cream
- Use stickers to place along the pre-writing lines
- Use wooden sticks or craft sticks to place on top of pre-writing lines
- Use fine motor tweezers to place cotton balls along pre-writing lines
- Cover the pre-writing line page with cornmeal and trace with a finger
- Use bath crayons on the bathtub or during a shower
- Use play dough to form pre-writing lines

- Squeeze glitter glue along pre-writing lines
- Use pip-cleaners to place along or form pre-writing lines.
- Use mini marshmallows and tooth picks to form letters or pre-writing lines
- Writing icing ice cubes on a chalk board
- Make cookie letters or pre-writing lines using a rolling pin.
- Trace letters or lines onto your child's back with your finger and have them guess which letter you wrote
- Make letters and lines with pipe cleaners or wikki stix.
- Form letters or lines with french fries
- Use a flashlight to make letters or lines/shapes on the wall
- Draw letters or lines/shapes on the carpet with your fingers
- Draw letters or lines/shapes outside with sidewalk chalk
- Make letters or lines/shapes with glue and cotton balls (draw the letter or line in glue on a piece of construction paper, then place the cotton balls on top to form each letter)
- Have your child lay on the floor and imitate letters or shapes with their bodies (example: curling into a circle for the letter "O", making their body look like a "S" and so on)

CHAPTER 10

Activity Ideas by Age

In this chapter you will find activity ideas divided by age. Remember, all activities should be done with adult supervision. Some activities may include smaller items, so use your own judgement when setting up activities for younger children who still put items in their mouth.

Fine Motor Activities for Ages 0-3

Activities at this age should be all about exploring new environments and items in order to build well rounded fine motor skills.

Tummy Time Activity Ideas

Here are some ways you can work some tummy time into your baby's day. I'll also list some ways you can use tummy time with older children if they missed tummy time as a baby. Keep in mind, any child can benefit from extended tummy time.

- Lay your baby on your chest facing towards you. Switch the position/side their head is on each time to avoid their heads becoming flat on one side.
- Lie on the floor with your baby, encouraging them to rest on their elbows and lift their head. Use gentle support of the torso and arms to help them be comfortable.
- Place toys on the floor around your baby so they can see them. This will encourage reaching, which will in turn promote raising of the head which strengthens neck and tummy muscles.
- While you are watching TV (remember that too much TV exposure is bad for your baby's eyesight) or talking with friends or family, drape your baby stomach down over your lap, patting their back for reassurance.

Crawling Activities

- Playing in tunnels
- Crawling under, over, or through an object (such as tables,

chairs)
- Placing a favorite item just out of reach and encouraging the baby to reach and crawl for it
- Show your baby how to crawl by doing it yourself
- Animal walks (18 months +)
- Learn to peddle a bike (closer to age 2)
- Climbing small ladders or play structures (18 months to age 2)

Fine Motor Activities for Ages 0-2 Years

- Grasping and letting go (rings, blocks, rattles, favorite blanket or stuffed animal).
- Turning objects in their hands Introducing new and novel toys will also encourage them to explore and turn that object in their hands to figure it out.
- Stacking blocks (for this age stacking 2-6 blocks is age appropriate).
- Drawing with crayons (do not use regular crayons at this age, rock crayons or triangle crayons work best).
- Snapping and buttoning (large or extra-large sized buttons).
- Taking items out and putting them into containers.
- Mess free painting in a sealed plastic bag.
- Finger foods during meal times.
- Bath toys during bath time (particularly ones that allow them to dump water).
- Music toys such as rattlers and bell shakers.
- Pushing blocks through a square or circle shaped hole.
- Turning the pages of a board book.
- Stringing 1/2 inch to 1 inch sized beads on string.
- Hand clapping games.
- Building with building blocks.

Fine Motor Activities for Ages 2-3 Years

Most children around this age have stopped putting objects in their mouths. Use your own judgement and always supervise all activities, especially those with smaller parts or smaller objects.

- Squeezing bottles such a ketchup with both hands.
- Rolling dough (either making bread, cookies, or play dough).
- Pressing cookie cutters into dough.
- Drawing pictures with a simple stencil outline.
- Putting rings or pegs on a peg board.
- Using play dough scissors to make snips in the dough.
- Simulate cutting by transferring objects with bubble tongs.
- Cut straws into pieces for a necklace.
- Cut out foam shapes.
- Complete simple 2-4 turn mazes (be sure they are steadying the paper with the opposite hand).
- Complete simple connect the dots (steadying the paper with the opposite hand).
- Folding paper in half.
- Squeezing spray bottles to water plants or clean windows.
- Complete lacing cards.
- Use tongs to pick up cotton balls, cereal pieces, rice, beans etc.
- Coloring or scribbling with age appropriate grasp.
- Roll play dough shapes such a horizontal or vertical lines, circle shapes etc.
- Squeeze plastic bottles or a turkey baster to transfer water.
- Squeeze play dough or putty.
- Pinch clothes pins.
- Draw shapes or lines in shaving cream or hair gel.
- Draw with an Etch-A-Sketch.
- Trace a simple pattern or design on paper.
- Use finger paint to practice lines and shapes.
- Put 3-4 piece puzzles together.
- Build a block tower (6-10 blocks high is age appropriate).
- Place pegs on a peg board.
- Put coins into a piggy bank.
- Scoop objects with a small spoon (rice, beans, small pasta etc).
- Screw and unscrew lids on containers.

- Put small objects into a container or cup.
- Count objects such a buttons, beads, cotton balls.
- Pound golf tees into a foam board with a hammer.
- Play in a ball pit.
- Water play with buckets, cups and other pouring items.
- Place strips of fabric in an empty wipes container and pull them out through the lid.
- Cooked spaghetti play using tongs and other fine motor tools.
- Sensory bin with objects for transferring and pouring.
- Make a sound box using rattles, drums, bells and other musical instruments.
- Make discovery bottles using water bottles (plastic is best since some children still throw items at this age).
- Make homemade play dough.
- Make homemade finger paint.
- Texture sticks for counting patterns.

Fine Motor Activities for Ages 3-6

Also known as the "preschool years", children this age are beginning to fine tune their movement and build on skills for future academic activities.

"Tummy Time" Activities for Preschoolers

You can still work on tummy time with preschoolers, it is especially important for those who did not get it often as a baby. Here are some ways you can do that.

- While working on pre-writing lines and shapes
- Completing Puzzles
- Using clips and stringing beads
- Coloring and drawing
- Reading
- Playing with cars or trucks

• While watching a movie, television, or using a tablet.

Also remember, it is important to provide lots of different positions for completing activities at this age. Sitting on a ball seat, standing, or kneeling are excellent ways to work on core strength and stability while adding in some fine motor skill practice.

Activities for Children Who Skipped Crawling

Any activity that involves bilateral coordination (especially using both the arms and legs together, will be a good activity for children who skipped crawling at a young age.

• Tunnel play

- Climbing
- Animals crawls and movements
- Riding a bike
- Monkey bars
- Rock climbing
- Yoga
- Swimming
- Martial Arts

Activity Ideas for Ages 3-6 Years

- Place pegs into peg boards.
- Complete lacing cards.
- Building with building blocks/bricks.
- Tear lettuce into pieces for a salad.
- Tear construction paper for a collage.
- Peeling stickers.
- Spread icing on cookies or cupcakes.
- Use both arms to twirl streamers.
- Making bead necklaces or bracelets.
- Putting up to 12 piece puzzles together.
- Cut straws into pieces and use to make a necklace.
- Complete 4-6 turn mazes.
- Cut out circle, triangle, and square shapes.
- Cut out clothes for stick people with craft sticks.
- Folding paper into fourths.
- Cutting with crinkle cut or design scissors.
- Threading buttons.
- Cut out colored lines and make a rainbow.
- Cutting yarn.
- Complete a cutting activity book.
- Use clothespins to pick up objects.
- Pinch fruit loops and slide over tooth picks.
- Form letters with Wikki Stix.
- Push beads onto pipe cleaners.

- Form lines and shapes with pipe cleaners.
- Use fine motor tweezers or tongs to pick up objects.
- Trace letters in shaving cream.
- Trace sandpaper letters.
- Use letter stamps to form their name.
- String letter beads to form their name.
- Use a hole punch to cut out designs.
- Button or unbutton large buttons on clothing or button board.
- Draw a person with at least 6 body parts included.
- Learn to tie their shoes.
- Build complex shapes (towers, bridges, pyramids, etc) with blocks.
- Screwing various size lids onto containers.
- Practice coloring within the lines.
- Tracing around their own hand with a pencil or crayon.
- Reeling a fishing pole.
- Simple food preparation (measuring, stirring, cutting soft items with a butter knife)
- Play with sensory bins.
- Finger painting.
- Popping large bubble wrap.
- Playing with bread dough or play dough.
- Planting flowers or plants in a garden.
- Drawing in sand.
- Washing dishes.
- Drawing or tracing in couscous, rice, lentils, shaving cream etc.
- Playing with musical instruments (drum, piano, violin, recorder, etc)

Fine Motor Activity Ideas for Ages 6+

Depending on your child's interest or abilities, many of the previous activities will still be beneficial for older children. Here are a list of more age appropriate activities that may interest older children.

- Art classes
- Gymnastics
- Yoga
- Swimming
- Roller blading or roller skating
- Team sports (such as baseball, football, soccer, hockey etc)
- Wrestling
- Tennis
- Horseback riding (especially grooming and pre-riding activities)
- Taking care of a pet (dog, cat, bird etc)
- Origami (paper folding art)
- Cooking and baking
- Music lessons (particularly piano, string, or woodwind instruments)
- Jewelry making
- Coloring books (those with more detailed designs)
- Puzzles (those with 50+ pieces or more detailed pictures)
- Dance
- Play croquet
- Crocheting
- Wood working
- Building
- Computer coding or building computers
- Mechanical work
- Board games
- Playing capture the flag

Final Thoughts

We have explored many topics in this journey of fine motor skill development. It is important to remember that all children develop at their own pace. I have found with my own children that activities I thought would interest one may not interest the other at all. Remember to have fun and let them naturally explore their world through the amazing senses and gifts they have been given.

Allowing your child the freedom to explore in hands-on ways is the best thing you can give them for their future success and independence. It does not need to be something elaborate. Focus on their interests and strengths, while finding ways to encourage them in skills they have difficulty with.

You may find your child struggles with a skill that you thought would come easy. It can be frustrating for everyone involved. As caregivers, it is our job to support and encourage our children to try again and strive to be the best they can be.

GLOSSARY OF TERMS

Asymmetrical tonic neck reflex - A reflex seen in the first 6-7 months of a baby's life: as the head turns to one side, the arm and leg extend on that same side to allow the baby to explore it visually. As the one side extends, the opposite side bends in or flexes.

Core strength – Activities or exercises that strengthen your "core" muscles such as back, abdominal, and around the pelvis.

Balance – The ability to use vestibular function, vision, and proprioception to maintain posture including coordinating motion of body parts, and modulate fine motor skills. Also includes the ability to maintain and control body position during static or dynamic positions.

Bilateral coordination – The ability to use both sides of the body together in a controlled and organized way. Using both sides of the brain together in order to coordinate body movements.

Body awareness - Knowing where the body and limbs are in space without looking at them.

Crossing midline – An imaginary line down the center of the body which allows a child to cross the middle of the body with the arms and legs over to the opposite side (such a drawing a horizontal line, reading across the page, or sitting cross-legged on the floor).

Dexterity – Skill in performing a task, particularly with the use of the hands.

Dynamic balance – The ability to maintain balance and control while engaged in movement.

Dynamic tripod grasp - The dynamic tripod grasp is considered the most efficient grasp for handwriting. It includes the thumb and index finger on a pencil with the middle finger placed on the side of the pencil. The last two fingers are curled slightly in the palm of the hand.

Eye-hand coordination – The ability to grasp and hold an object while looking at it. Using the eyes and hands together.

Fine motor skills – The ability to use and control the small muscles of the hand, arm, and fingers for things such as grasping, holding, writing, dressing, and more.

Functional visual skills - Visual skills such as eye tracking and convergence needed for reading and writing.

Grasping reflex - When you grab a baby's hand or fingers and they automatically grasp around your finger or hand.

Gross motor skills – The ability to control large muscle groups such as legs, trunk/torso, back, and abdomen for activities such as crawling, running, sitting, standing, and walking.

Handwriting skills - A complex skill of using language by pencil grip, letter formation, and body posture. There are many skills involved in handwriting including vision, eye-hand coordination, muscle memory, posture, body control, as well as pencil grasp and letter formation.

Motor planning - Ability for the brain to organize incoming sensory information and respond to carry out a new motor skill with accuracy.

Muscle memory – Repetition of one action which allows that action to be memorized and performed without much effort.

Muscle tone - The state of muscle fiber tension between the different muscles and muscle groups. The degree of muscle tension or resistance during rest in response to stretching.

Quadruped grasp – A 4 fingered grasp with the writing tool held between the thumb, index and middle finger. Movement happens at the wrist, hand and fingers and it moves as one movement.

Palmar grasp – An infant primitive grasp that allows them to hold an object with their palm and wrapping the fingers and thumb around an **object from one side.**

Pincer grasp – Using the thumb and index finger in order to grasp or "pinch" objects between their fingers.

Pre-writing skills - The prerequisite for handwriting skills which involves being able to hold a writing utensil appropriately and tracing or copying lines and shapes needed to form letters.

Proprioception - An internal senses of the body that comes from the joints, muscles, ligaments, and other connective tissue. The proprioception system allows you to know where your body parts are and what they are doing without necessarily looking at them.

Raking grasp - A grasp seen around 7-8 months age where a child grasps objects using all their fingers and hand except the thumb.

Reflexes - An automatic response to sensory stimuli.

Rooting reflex - When a baby automatically turns towards stimuli and starts to make a sucking noise and movements. Particularly crucial to infant feeding and future motor development for turning towards a toy and rolling.

Startle (moro) reflex - Also known as the Moro Reflex, is common in baby's up to 3-4 months old. It involves the baby reaching both arms out wide (abduction), un-spreading the arms (adduction), and crying. It is a protective reflex when a baby feels like it is falling or unstable.

Static tripod grasp – There are two types of tripod grasps, dynamic tripod and static tripod grasp. The thumb and index finger are placed on the writing utensil

Sucking reflex - A hand-to-mouth reflex that goes along with sucking. Baby's will often suck their fingers or hands while this reflex is present.

Trunk control – The ability to align the body for activities such as walking, running, and jumping.

Tummy time – Placing an infant or baby of 6 months and under on their stomach in encourage neck, abdomen, and trunk muscle strength and development. Children who are older also benefit from "tummy time" activities if they lack strong trunk and core strength.

Vestibular system - The vestibular system is located in the inner ear and helps you to detect changes in regards to gravity. Offend referred to as the body's GPS system.

Visual discrimination - The ability to recognize visual images. Allows you to identify and recognize different shapes, forms, colors, objects, people, and printed materials.

Visual-motor integration - When motor skills work together with the eye or vision to form eye-hand coordination. Both systems must be integrated for many fine motor and handwriting skills.

Visual-motor skills - Combining visual perceptual skills, functional visual skills, and eye-hand coordination.

Visual-perceptual skills - The ability organize and interpret visual information and give it meaning. Needed for reading, spelling, math comprehension, and handwriting skills.

Resources

These are some of my favorite websites and places for find more information on fine motor skills. If you would like to see even more resources with clickable links for each, visit: www.GrowingHandsOnKids.com/FineMotorResources

Websites & Therapy Blogs

www.TheOTToolbox.com - Lots of fine motor and handwriting information and activity ideas written by an Occupational Therapist.

www.MamaOT.com - A focus on child development and easy activities for parents and therapists to use that work on skills needed for everyday activities. Lots of great information for new grads.

www.TheInspiredTreehouse.com - Written by an Occupational Therapist and Physical Therapist, this site focuses on sensory processing and child development, as well as easy and fun activities for gross motor, fine motor, and visual motor skills. Also co-authors of the book Sensory Processing 101 and many other resources in their shop.

www.PocketOT.com - This site focuses on sensory processing and information particularly for Autism Spectrum Disorders, written by an Occupational Therapist. Also the author of two great books, The Weighted Blanket Guide and The Special Needs School Survival Guide.

www.TherapyFunZone.net - Written by an Occupational Therapist, this site features lots of hands-on and easy to put together fine motor activities for kids of all ages. You can also find the Munchy Ball fine motor tool in her shop.

www.KidsPlaySmarter.com - This site focuses on fine motor, gross motor, handwriting, sensory processing, and therapist tips written by an Occupational Therapist.

www.YourTherapySource.com - This site has lots of printable and hand-outs that focus on fine motor, handwriting, sensory processing, and visual motor activities written by an Occupational Therapist.

www.YourKidsOT.com - This site is for parents, educators and therapists interested in providing creative learning opportunities for kids. You will find Occupational Therapy terminology explained and information about how an OT can help your child. Also written by an Occupational Therapist.

www.KidsPlaySpace.com - This site is dedicated to providing simple learning opportunities every day. You will find everything you need to know about play, play spaces, play resources and more. Written by an Occupational Therapist.

www.OT-Mom-Learning-Activities.com - This site focuses on all the skills children need to function in the school environment. She is also a homeschooling mom of three and an Occupational Therapist.

www.ToolstoGrowOT.com - This site caters to therapists and provides a membership site and handouts focusing on fine motor skills, bilateral coordination, visual perception, visual motor integration, sensory processing, handwriting, executive functioning, self-care/life skills, gross motor skills and more. Written by two Occupational Therapists.

www.CanDoKiddo.com - This site focuses on baby and young toddler development, including milestones, baby gear reviews, feeding, and easy activities to promote fine motor skills. Written by a Occupational Therapist who specializes in early intervention.

www.MissJaimeOT.com - This site focuses on easy and fun activities and resources for sensory processing, fine motor skills, handwriting, motor skills, and visual perception skills for kids of all ages. Written by an Occupational Therapist.

www.HandwritingWithKatherine.com - This site focusing on handwriting skills for children all ages and abilities. Written by an Occupational Therapist.

Non-Therapy Blogs

These sites or blogs are written by teachers, parents/moms, or other professionals and have a large focus on fine motor activities. There are so many out there, these are just a few of my favorites. To find the fine motor activities, search each website below for "fine motor skills" or "fine motor activities"

www.ToddlerApproved.com

www.Teaching2And3YearOlds.com

www.Pre-KPages.com

www.TeachingMama.org

www.PowerfulMothering.com

www.MamasHappyHive.com

www.TheImaginationTree.com

www.HandsOnAsWeGrow.com

www.HappyHooligans.com

www.LalyMom.com

www.MessForLess.com

www.AndNextComesL.com

www.TheMeasuredMom.com

www.LittleBinsForLittleHands.com

www.ThisReadingMama.com

www.GiftofCuriosity.com

www.HowWeeLearn.com

www.NaturalBeachLiving.com

www.LivingMontessoriNow.com

Favorites Shops and Products

The Handwriting Book - Written by 10 pediatric Occupational and Physical Therapists with everything you need to know about handwriting in one handy ebook. **www.FunctionalSkillsforKids.com**

Fundanoodle - An early learning readiness company with products designed by Pediatric Occupational Therapists for children of all abilities ages preschool through 2nd grade. A multi-sensory approach with products that focus on the gross motor, visual motor and fine motor skills needed for successful handwriting in the home, school or therapy practice. **http://MyFundanoodle.com/GrowingHandsOnKids**

The Pencil Grip Inc. - This site specializes in handwriting and pencil grips such as The Pinch Grip, The Crossover Grip, and the Writing Claw. **www.ThePencilGrip.com**

Ark Therapeutic Inc. - This store specializes in sensory processing chews and fidgets and also created the Tran-Quill® Writing Kit (Vibrating pencil and pen). **www.ArkTherapeutic.com**

Adapt-Ease - Occupational therapy designed tools and toys on Amazon. Search Amazon for "Adapt-Ease" to find their products.

Therapy Shoppe® - A therapy product supply store for the classroom, home, or therapy practice. **www.TherapyShoppe.com**

Fun And Function - A therapy product supply store that focuses on special needs toys and products. **www.FunAndFunction.com**

Melissa & Doug - Hands-on learning toys that include functional activities and real wooden materials. **www.MelissaAndDoug.com** (also on Amazon)

Resource Citations

TBergmann, K. (1990). Incidence of atypical pencil grasps among non-dysfunctional adults. American Journal of Occupational Therapy, 44, 736-740

Blank Children's Hospital - Iowa Health System. Tummy Time with Your Baby. www.BlankChildrens.org

Brain Balance Center. Retained Primitive Reflexes as a Sign of Brain Imbalance. https://www.BrainBalanceCenters.com/blog/2014/09/retained-primitive-reflexes-sign-brain-imbalance/

Breslin, D., & Exner, C. (1999). Construct validity of the in-hand manipulation test: A discriminant analysis with children without disability and children with spastic diplegia. American Journal of Occupational Therapy, 53(4), 381-386

Burton, W., & Dancisak, J. (2000). Grip form and graphomotor control in preschool children. American Journal of Occupational Therapy, 54(1), 9-17.

Cameron, C. E., Brock, L. L., Murrah, W. M., Bell, L. H., Worzalla, S. L., Grissmer, D., & Morrison, F. J. (2012). Fine Motor Skills and Executive Function Both Contribute to Kindergarten Achievement. Child Development, 83(4), 1229-1244. doi: 10.1111/j.1467-8624.2012.01768.x
http://OnlineLibrary.Wiley.com/doi/10.1111/j.1467-8624.2012.01768.x/abstract

Case-Smith, J. (1993). Comparison of in-hand manipulation skills in children with and without fine motor delays. Occupational Therapy Journal of Research, 13(2), 87-100

Clark, Gloria Jean, "The relationship between handwriting, reading, fine motor and visual-motor skills in kindergarteners" (2010). Graduate Theses and Dissertations. Paper 11399.

Cranial Technologies. Babies & Tummy Time – Understanding the importance of Tummy Time. June 1 2005. www.CranialTechnologies.com

Dennis, J., & Swinth, Y. (2001). Pencil grasp and children's handwriting legibility during different-length writing tasks. American Journal of Occupational Therapy, 55(2), 175-183.

Innovations in Education. Fine Motor Skills, Handwriting, or Writing? What's the Difference? 2012. Innovations in Education Blog. https://InnovationsEd.Wordpress.com/2012/08/17/fine-motor-skills-handwriting-or-writing-whats-the-difference/

Jennings PT MA, Judy. Lucht MPH, OTR/L, Peggy. Parent Workshop On Readiness Skills. May, 2006. www.Fit-Baby.com

Kelly, Kate. How Sensory Processing Issues Can Affect Fine Motor Skills. Understood. https://www.Understood.org/en/learning-attention-issues/child-learning-disabilities/sensory-processing-issues/how-sensory-processing-issues-can-affect-motor-skills

Primary Children's Hospital. Let's Talk About… Tummy Time. Intermountain Healthcare. 2016.

Promislow, Sharon, Educational Kinesiology. Making the Brain Body Connection: A Playful Guide to Releasing Mental, Physical, and Emotional Blocks to Success. 2005.

Roston, K., Hinojosa, J., & Kaplan, H. (2008). Using the Minnesota Handwriting Assessment and the handwriting checklist in screening first and second graders' handwriting legibility. Journal of Occupational Therapy, Schools & Early Intervention, 1, 100-115.

Stevens L (2004) Hands up! Handwriting skills resource book, Handwriting Project, Torrensville Primary School, Participatory Community Practice, University of South Australia, Division of Health Sciences, School of Health Sciences, Adelaide.

Skill Builders. Fine Motor Development 0 to 6 Years. 2002 Skill Builders Online.

Smith, Barbara, A. MS, OTR/L. From Rattles to Writing - A Parent's Guide to Hand Skills. 2011. Therapro. Inc.

Ziviani, J., & Wallen, M. (2006). The development of graphomotor skills. In A. Henderson & C. Pehoski (Eds.), Hand function in the child: Foundations for remediation (2nd ed.) (pp. 217-236). St. Louis, MO: Mosby.

Ziviani, J., & Wilkins, J. (1986). Effects of pencil grip on handwriting speed and legibility. Education Review, 38, 247-257.

About the Author

Heather Greutman is a Certified Occupational Therapy Assistant and graduated in 2006. She now stays home with her two children (ages 4 and 1) and writes on her therapy/homeschool mom site, Growing Hands-On Kids. Encouraging independence, one activity at a time is the main theme of her site and she shares information on child development, Occupational therapy tips, special needs, homeschooling, and hands-on activity ideas that focus on ages 0-6. She also enjoys photography, a good period drama on Netflix and coffee. Heather lives in Cincinnati, Ohio with her husband David and children.

To find more resources like this one from Growing Hands-On Kids, please visit: **shop.GrowingHandsOnKids.com**

Looking for printable hand-outs to share with your friends, teachers, therapists, or parents?

Get a fine motor printable bundle of all the developmental checklists, activity suggestions, and other shareable resources from this book.

Visit: **www.GrowingHandsOnKids.com/FineMotorBundle**